MAL

CELTIC CROSSES
OF BRITAIN
AND IRELAND

SHIRE ARCHAEOLOGY

Cover photograph
Cross of Muiredach, Monasterboice, County Louth, Ireland.
(Author's photograph.)

British Library Cataloguing in Publication Data:
Seaborne, Malcolm.
Celtic crosses of Britain and Ireland
(Shire Archaeology; 57).
1. Great Britain. Stone crosses.
I. Title.
736'.5.
ISBN 0-7478-0003-0.

Published in 1994 by
SHIRE PUBLICATIONS LTD,
Cromwell House, Church Street, Princes Risborough,
Aylesbury, Bucks HP17 9AJ, UK.

Series Editor: James Dyer.

ISBN 0 7478 0003 0.

First published 1989.
Reprinted with corrections 1994.

Printed in Great Britain by
CIT Printing Services,
Press Buildings, Merlins Bridge, Haverfordwest, Dyfed SA61 1XF.

Contents

4

List of illustrations

Introduction

The subject of the stone crosses of the early Christian period was examined in great detail by a number of Victorian and Edwardian antiquarians. Their interpretations have been modified or expanded since but it was they who laid the foundations of modern studies of the subject. By carefully recording the examples which had survived and by rescuing many fragments which had fallen into neglect, they ensured that a vast corpus of material remains available to the modern student. J. Romilly Allen examined crosses in many areas and published his massive *Early Christian Monuments of Scotland* in 1903. Equally thorough were A. G. Langdon's *Old Cornish Crosses* (1896) and P. M. C. Kermode's *Manx Crosses* (1907). These were later followed by V. E. Nash-Williams's authoritative volume on *The Early Christian Monuments of Wales* (1950) and the detailed studies of the Irish crosses undertaken by Françoise Henry, some of whose works, together with those of more recent scholars in this field, are listed in the bibliography.

Given the large amount of material available, this short study can do no more than refer to some of the best preserved examples and to explore selected aspects of their complex development. Although the focus will be on the Celtic areas to the west, the period in which these crosses were made was one of many cultural influences and cross-currents, which were reflected in the sculpture created. Ringed and disc-headed crosses in stone were distinctive of the Celtic areas and spread to parts of Anglo-Danish England and further afield. The tall free-standing cross was a development common to Celtic and Anglo-Saxon art but appears to have been less popular on the continent of Europe, apart from Brittany (itself a Celtic enclave), where crosses were later added to some of the prehistoric menhirs which abound there. It was the combination of the ringed head and the high cross which produced the best known type of Celtic cross, but it will be shown that many other cross-forms and iconographic themes were used during the period between the conversion of the Celts to Christianity and the Norman conquest. Taken as a whole, the incised and sculptured crosses of this period are among the most compelling expressions of early Christian art.

What was the purpose of these monuments? Primarily they were a testimony to the Christian faith of the unknown persons who erected them. In only a minority of cases can it be proved that they marked burials. Many of the later crosses were erected to bear witness to a general faith in Christianity, while serving subsidiary purposes such as marking the precinct of a monastery or a place associated with the founder of a particular community, or illustrating aspects of the biblical story which seemed to the people at the time particularly worth stressing. Owing to the lack of detailed information about contemporary contexts and the well known difficulty of dating early Christian sculpture, it is not possible to do more than indicate broad periods and groupings. Nevertheless, it is hoped that the descriptions given in this book, and the publications listed at the end, will enable the reader to discover some of the answers to the question of how these monuments came to be created.

Acknowledgements

In Scotland Mr Michael Spearman of the Royal Museum in Edinburgh was very helpful, and in Ireland I enjoyed the hospitality of Dr Kenneth Milne and was also helped by Miss Felicity Devlin of the National Museum in Dublin. In Wales, the staff of the National Museum in Cardiff gave me every assistance, and I am particularly grateful to Canon Wyn Evans of Trinity College, Carmarthen, who was kind enough to read my typescript and to suggest a number of improvements. In Cornwall, I benefited from the help of Canon R. M. Catling and of Mr R. D. Penhallurick of the Cornwall County Museum at Truro. The staff of the Manx Museum in Douglas were similarly helpful. I am grateful to all the copyright holders who gave permission for their photographs to be reproduced and to the incumbents of churches and curators of museums who allowed me to take photographs. The photographs not otherwise credited are mine and I am especially grateful to my son Michael for printing my negatives. My thanks are also due to Mrs Christine Lynas, who typed my manuscript with her usual efficiency.

1
Cross-decorated stones

The cross is now the universal symbol of Christianity but it was some centuries before it came to be adopted. It is, for example, very rare on the wall paintings in the Catacombs and it seems that the association of the cross with crucifixion and persecution was considered by the first Christians to be best avoided. They preferred to show the figure of the Good Shepherd or to use symbols such as the peacock or the fish. During the fourth century and for several centuries thereafter the chi-rho monogram was the preferred symbol (see figure 1).

The emperor Constantine issued an edict of toleration of Christianity in the Roman empire following his victory at the battle of the Milvian Bridge in 312. During this battle he used the *labarum* on his standard, which consisted of the first two letters of the Greek word for Christ, surrounded by a wreath of victory. The Greek letter for 'Ch' was like our modern X and the 'r' like our modern P. The wreath was often represented as a circle, and so the earliest monogram was as shown in figure 1 (a), a form found, for example, on the mosaic floor in the Roman villa at Hinton St Mary, Dorset, now in the British Museum, and on a number of objects originating in the fourth century, such as the Water Newton collection of silver also in the British Museum. The uniting of the X and the P to form a plus sign with a loop, as shown in figure 1 (b), seems to have been a late fourth- and fifth-century development. It was this form, and the later modification of it in which the upper part of the P was left open to make a shape like a shepherd's crook, as in figure 1 (c), which are found on some of the earliest Christian stones in Celtic Britain and Ireland. It is also probable that the simple ring-cross, as in figure 1 (d), often with a stem attached, which was very widely used on early Christian incised stones, was derived from the

1. The development of the chi-rho monogram: (a) original form; (b) X and P united; (c) hooked P; (d) ring-cross.

chi-rho.

The earliest carved stones with Christian associations which survive in the Celtic west date from the fifth, sixth and seventh centuries. This is the period often called the 'Age of the Saints'. There is good evidence that the diocesan structure of the late Roman empire survived in those parts of Wales and northern Britain which were least affected by the Anglo-Saxon invasions. Professor Charles Thomas has argued that it was probably the sub-Roman diocese of Carlisle which sent Ninian to Whithorn in Galloway early in the fifth century and may have been the milieu from which Patrick was carried off to Ireland, from where he escaped to return again in 432 (or 456 according to some scholars) to spread the gospel. In Wales the work of sixth-century saints such as David and Illtud in the south and Deiniol in the north is indirectly attested by the many early Christian inscribed stones of this period, which also provide evidence of continuing contact between Wales, Cornwall, Ireland and other Christian communities in Gaul. The inscriptions were carved on natural boulders or slabs, either in Latin or in oghams, a method of cutting notches on the edge of the stone thought to have been invented in southern Ireland in the fourth century. There are over three hundred ogham-inscribed stones in Ireland, concentrated in the south, and, although it was considered that these were of pagan origin, it has more recently been suggested that they may have been associated with the very earliest pre-Patrick church in Ireland. The ogham inscriptions on mainland Britain are indicative of the presence of Irish settlers, and in these areas ogham markings on the edge of the stone are sometimes accompanied by the same inscription in Latin letters, arranged vertically like the oghams.

These earliest stones are particularly numerous in Wales, where the 139 examples recorded and classified by Nash-Williams as Group I stones have been increased to about 150 by subsequent discoveries. There are also about fifty in Cornwall and Devon, about a dozen in what is now the south of Scotland and half a dozen on the Isle of Man. A small number of these early inscribed stones bear the chi-rho monogram and three examples are illustrated here. Figure 2, which may now be seen on a stone fixed to an inside wall of the church at Penmachno in Gwynedd, has the chi-rho form shown in figure 1 (b) but without a circle. The inscription reads CARAVSIVS/HIC IACIT/IN HOC CON/ GERIES LA/PIDVM, that is 'Carausius lies here in this heap of stones'. It is dated to the fifth or early sixth century. Like most of

2. (Left) 'Carausius' pillar-stone, Penmachno, Gwynedd.
3. (Right) Pillar-stone, Kirkmadrine, Galloway.

these early inscribed stones, it does not now occupy its original position and only a small proportion of them can be proved to have been found in association with burials. It is possible that many of them were set up some considerable time after the death of the person commemorated and may have served to mark a boundary or for some purpose other than marking a grave. Shown in figure 3 is one of a group of three early pillar-stones of massive size now preserved in the glass-fronted porch of the nineteenth-century chapel at Kirkmadrine on the Rhins peninsula in Galloway (together with a number of other early cross-inscribed stones from that area). The stone illustrated has the later open rho but preserves the circle. Very common additions to the monogram were the Greek letters alpha and omega, and in this example the words INITIUM ET FINIS, 'the beginning and the end', are carved below the monogram.

4. (Left) 'Irneit' cross-slab, Maughold, Isle of Man. (Photograph: Manx Museum and National Trust.)

5. (Right) Pillar-stone, Reask, County Kerry. (Photograph: Commissioners of Public Works, Ireland.)

Our last example (figure 4) is a cross-slab from Maughold on the Isle of Man and is of somewhat later date (late seventh or eighth century). Here the monogram has been replaced by a hexafoil pattern within circles which were probably set out with a compass. A vestigial rho-loop survives on the top of the incised crosses below the circle. The inscription within the circle, in debased Roman letters, records a Celtic bishop called Irneit. Geometrical patterns using compass arcs were relatively common at this period and another notable example may be seen in the museum at Whithorn in Galloway — the 'St Peter' stone, which also dates from the seventh century and has a rho-loop on one arc.

Clearly, these earliest cross-forms appearing in the Celtic areas were based on imported models. These forms would have been familiar to the early Christians in the west from easily transportable objects such as jewellery, pilgrims' flasks and pottery. One of the Mediterranean imports found during the excavation of Dinas Emrys in Gwynedd was a pottery roundel (part of a lamp, now in the National Museum of Wales) with a chi-rho symbol marked on it. Contact between Wales and Christian communities in Gaul has also been cited for some of the Latin formulae used on the early inscribed stones. The chi-rho form was, however, considerably elaborated in the succeeding centuries and it is also clear that simple Latin or Greek crosses either developed from the chi-rho monogram or were introduced independently. An outstanding example of adaptation to indigenous traditions may be seen on the pillar-stone at Reask in County Kerry, Ireland (figure 5). In this case spirals were skilfully incised to produce a balanced composition which also makes use of the naturally uneven surface of the stone. Here again we have a cross of arcs, with the letters DNE (for *Domine*, Lord) set vertically. Dr Henry suggests a seventh-century date for this stone.

From the seventh century onwards there are numerous examples of cross-decorated stones, usually without inscriptions and showing cross-patterns of many varieties. The Welsh examples were classified by Nash-Williams as 'Group II' stones dating from the seventh to the ninth centuries and many other examples have survived in Ireland, parts of Scotland and the Isle of Man. Because of the lack of inscriptions they are very difficult to date with accuracy and stones with simple crosses could have continued to be carved well into the medieval period. Many of them have been gathered together in museums or later church buildings and their original context is unknown. It is therefore difficult to determine the exact purpose for which they were used. A certain number have been recognised as fragments of architectural features or panels of shrines, coffins or altars, which shed valuable light on early liturgical practices. Many of these stones were no doubt grave-markers and concentrations of them probably indicate the beginnings of Christian cemeteries, perhaps at first only for monks or clergy.

Stones bearing only an incised cross vary in size from beach pebble stones (such as may be seen in the Whithorn Museum),

6. Pillar-stone, Llangernyw, Clwyd.

which may have been placed over, or even in, the grave, to tall standing stones with relatively small crosses. One such stone may be seen in the churchyard at Llangernyw in Clwyd (figure 6). Here a rough pillar-stone has been carved with an incised cross potent (that is with 'crutches' at the end of each arm) and dots, probably copied from a manuscript source. The form of the cross indicates a date between the seventh and ninth centuries.

The Llangernyw stone raises a further point. Without the cross it could be mistaken for a prehistoric menhir or standing stone, such as were common in the Celtic west. The *Tripartite Life* of St Patrick describes the saint cutting a cross on a stone which had been venerated by the pagan inhabitants of the area. The evidence for crosses later carved on prehistoric stones in Britain or Ireland is very slight (unlike Brittany) but it is likely that some of the earliest Christian monuments in the west were influenced by megalithic traditions. There is also considerable evidence of early Christian burials on prehistoric sites. On the other hand, it is thought that new techniques of carving in stone had to be learnt by the Celtic groups who adopted Christian beliefs and practices. Thus it is possible to trace a development from incised carvings to 'sunken' and 'false-relief' work and finally to fully modelled sculpture. The rate of such development, however, varied from place to place so that, for example, incised work is not necessarily an indication of early date.

It has often been suggested that the earliest crosses were made of wood, which has not survived. Some early cross-forms carved on stone appear to imitate wood, as with the outline cross which was re-used on a buttress of the church at Llangeinwen in Anglesey (figure 7). This has a spiked foot comparable, it has been suggested, with those on wooden crosses which were inserted in the ground. Later on, with the development of free-standing 'high' crosses, mortice and tenon joints were used with stone, perhaps based on woodworking techniques.

The cross-decorated stones with which this chapter is concerned only very rarely show human or animal figures. The early church, as we have seen, was slow to adopt the cross as its symbol and representations of the Crucifixion appear relatively late in Christian art. It appears on an ivory casket in fifth-century Italy but seems to be depicted rarely in manuscripts until the sixth

7. Outline cross re-used on buttress, Llangeinwen, Anglesey, Gwynedd.

8. (Left) Pillar-stone from Over Kirkhope, Ettrick, Borders, now in the Royal Museum of Scotland, Edinburgh. (Photograph: Royal Museum of Scotland.)

9. (Right) Pillar-cross, St Buryan, Cornwall. (Photograph: Royal Commission on Historical Monuments, England.)

century or in other media before the seventh and eighth. Human figures on the early stones tend to be confined to incised drawings of 'orans' figures, that is with both hands raised in the ancient attitude of prayer. There are several examples in Wales and Ireland and one on the stone from Over Kirkhope, now in the Royal Museum of Scotland, which is thought to commemorate a hermit who lived in the remote Ettrick hills south of Galashiels (see figure 8). In Cornwall, where there are many early inscribed stones but very few cross-slabs, it has been suggested that the iconography of some of the later free-standing crosses might have developed from the carved figures which may be seen at such places as St Buryan, near Land's End (figure 9).

There is, however, a small number of stones in Wales and Ireland which show unusual developments in inscribed figure work during this period. The first is the stone from Llywel near Trecastle in Powys, now in the British Museum. One face has an inscription in Latin and ogham and is dated to the fifth or early sixth century. The stone was later reset in the ground head downwards and the uninscribed face decorated with incised symbols or pictographs grouped in three panels, as shown in figure 10, from a cast in the Brecknock Museum. These pictographs have been interpreted as representing various Christian scenes and doctrines and the figure in the bottom panel is taken to be a bishop with his crozier. However, the style most closely resembles pre-Christian art in Brittany and the carving could perhaps have been carried out by someone returning from that Celtic province.

Our final example is one of a small group of stone slabs on the west coast of Ireland which have incised drawings of the Crucifixion. Dr Henry dates the slabs at Inishkea North and Duvillaun, both in County Mayo, to the late seventh century. The

10. Cast of Llywel stone, Brecknock Museum, Brecon, Powys.

11. Incised slab, Inishkea North, County Mayo. (Photograph: Commissioners of Public Works, Ireland.)

first of these is shown in figure 11. This is a remarkable stone which stands on a small island on what was then the extreme edge of the Christian world, though no doubt in touch with it by sea. The technique is crude but the iconography quite advanced. Here is the Crucifixion with the lance-bearer and sponge-bearer on each side, as were commonly shown on Crucifixion scenes of this period and later. It will be noted that Christ is shown wearing only a loincloth. The semi-naked Christ is in the Roman tradition of Christian art and other early representations of the Crucifixion in Ireland more usually show Christ robed in a *colobium*, which was the Byzantine model. We will, however, meet this type of Crucifixion again on some of the later cross-slabs of Wales.

2
Cross-slabs of Scotland and the Isle of Man

The Picts living in the part of Britain north of the Forth and Clyde are thought to have been a mixture of early Celtic settlers from Europe and of the original iron age inhabitants. The evidence provided by the ogham-inscribed stones for Irish settlements in Cornwall, Wales and the Isle of Man has been described, and a similar movement took place when the Scotti from Ulster began to settle in the area now known as Argyll and the Western Isles to form the kingdom of Dalriada. The link with Ireland was strengthened after the foundation of an Irish monastery at Iona in 563 and by the missionary activities of Columba and his disciples, who preached in Pictland and Northumbria and further afield. Pictish art was much influenced by that of Northumbria, which occupied what is now southern Scotland during the seventh century. The response of the Picts to Christianity also compares in an interesting way with that of the other Celtic areas to the west. There was much interaction between the artistic forms adopted in Scotland, Ireland and the Isle of Man, and this was further enhanced by the union of the Scottish and Pictish kingdoms in 843.

During the period when the early Christian communities in Wales and Ireland were carving incised crosses on undressed slabs and boulders, the Picts were incising their unique symbols on natural stones to produce the magnificent 'symbol stones' which make up Romilly Allen's Class I stones of Scotland. Scholars disagree about the date of these stones (the majority favouring the seventh century) and also about the extent to which the Picts were influenced by Christianity during the period of the Class I stones. What is certain is that from the eighth century onwards the Picts adopted the Christian cross as the central feature of their famous cross-slabs, which included representations of biblical as well as secular subjects. These slabs were carefully shaped and both sides were carved, often in relief. These are the Class II stones of Romilly Allen's detailed treatise, 'erect cross-slabs or recumbent coped stones with symbols and Celtic ornament sculptured in relief', and they are generally considered to date from the mid eighth to the mid ninth century. These were succeeded by cross-slabs and free-standing crosses from which the Pictish symbols were entirely absent (Class III).

Taken together, Class II and III stones are among the most impressive manifestations of early Christian art. Equally impressive are some of the cross-slabs carved during this period in the Isle of Man.

Controversy still continues about the meaning of the Class I symbol stones, which are not our concern here. With the Pictish cross-slabs of Class II and III the Christian symbolism is more comprehensible, though the function of these monuments — whether they marked burials and/or ecclesiastical sites — remains uncertain. Undoubtedly, however, they provide evidence of a thriving Christian culture, with schools of skilled masons at work, probably using pattern books. By choosing to develop the cross-slab, rather than the free-standing cross of Northumbria and Ireland, the Pictish carvers had more room to exercise their native talent for incised and, increasingly, relief work in stone. Their cross-slabs have often been compared with the 'carpet' pages of some contemporary illuminated manuscripts, and examples of some of the designs of the crosses which formed the main feature of their cross-slabs may be found on ornamental pages in the Book of Durrow, the Lindisfarne Gospels and the Lichfield Gospels.

It seems certain that the Pictish craftsmen had access to illustrations from manuscript sources, including early bestiaries or stories about mythical beasts, as well as those about St Paul, the first hermit in Egypt, and St Anthony, the patriarch of monks. They also adopted with enthusiasm a great variety of interlace patterns, which were used to add interest to the crosses outlined on the slabs, together with key and spiral patterns on some of the stones. The animal carvings on the Class I stones are justly famous, and the same vigour was shown in those depicted on the Class II stones. Some are naturalistic and the Picts showed a particular fondness for horsemen and hunting scenes, the most celebrated being that on the Hilton of Cadboll stone, now in the Royal Museum of Scotland in Edinburgh. The scenes depicted on the slabs which survive in many parts of eastern Scotland give a vivid insight into contemporary dress and other aspects of life during the eighth and ninth centuries. Other animal drawings, however, are of grotesque creatures, whose limbs are often attenuated to form intricate patterns.

It is generally agreed that, superlative as many of the designs are, the detail was not always fully understood and that Pictish art was highly eclectic in its choice of subjects. The usual cross-form adopted was the Latin cross with the angles between the shaft and the cross-bar either rounded or formed into double squares. Less frequently the cross was ringed, either in imitation of cross-forms from further west or perhaps of wooden crosses with struts supporting the arms. Another interesting variation was what has been termed the quadrilobate ring, where circles drawn through the rounded angles give a ring-like effect. There were many minor variations but the four main types are illustrated in figure 12.

The photograph of the cross-slab at Rossie Priory, Tayside (figure 13), illustrates some of these points. Here we see the 'page in stone', complete with border and interlaced cross and with rounded angles at the intersection of the cross. This slab is unusual in showing older Pictish symbols on the front with the cross; in most cases these were relegated to the back of the slab.

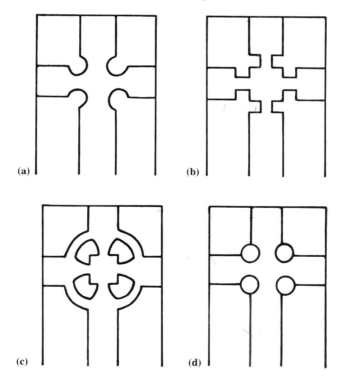

12. Cross-forms used on Pictish slabs: (a) rounded angles; (b) double-square angles; (c) partially rounded angles with ring; (d) quadrilobate ring.

13. Cross-slab, Rossie Priory, Tayside. (Photograph: Royal Commission on Ancient Monuments, Scotland.)

In this case, however, two of the most widely used of the earlier symbols appear on the left-hand side of the cross. (These are the crescent and V-rod, with the so-called 'elephant' symbol below.) In the bottom left-hand corner is a two-headed beast and in the top left-hand corner is a man grasping the necks of two other creatures. The only figure with Christian associations (apart from the cross itself) is the angel with outspread wings shown in the top right-hand corner. What is perhaps most remarkable about this slab is that, although a pattern may have been followed, there is nothing stereotyped about the draughtsmanship, while the diagonal arrangement of the horsemen, marching through the cross, is brilliantly conceived.

Our next two examples illustrate other points. The cross-slab in the churchyard at Aberlemno in Tayside (figure 14) shows the quadrilobate ring and also the development of fantastic animal decoration to form intricate patterns. The cross itself stands proud of the background and, as Dr Isabel Henderson has remarked of some of the Pictish cross-slabs, this gives an architectural presence similar to that of a free-standing cross. It is in many ways surprising that the Picts never experimented with the free-standing cross, though some were erected in what had previously been Pictish territory after the union with the Scots. It

14. Cross-slab, Aberlemno, Tayside. (Photograph: Royal Commission on Ancient Monuments, Scotland.)

15. (Left) Cross-slab, Dunfallandy, Tayside. (Photograph: Royal Commission on Ancient Monuments, Scotland.)

16. (Right) Back of cross-slab, Meigle, Tayside. (Photograph: Royal Commission on Ancient Monuments, Scotland.)

is also notable that representations of the Crucifixion, and New Testament scenes in general, were totally avoided on Class II stones.

With the cross-slab at Dunfallandy in Tayside (figure 15) we find a variation of the usual rounded-angled form of the cross and the addition of bosses on the arms, which are thought to have been imitated from metalwork. This was a feature which became very prominent on some later cross-slabs and may have spread from Pictland to Iona and Ireland (some scholars have argued that the route may have been in the opposite direction). The figures carved on this cross show the eclectic nature of much Pictish decoration. Beginning in the top left-hand corner and proceeding clockwise, there are panels of varying size with the following subjects: a beast with a human face, a beast standing over another beast, an angel with four wings, another angel, a beast with a reptile head, a beast biting its own tail, a monster swallowing a man, a stag with another beast above, and finally a beast with its head turned back. The monster swallowing a man is generally interpreted as a representation of Jonah and the whale, since it was usual in early Christian art to show the whale with an animal head (and sometimes legs) and a fish tail. In the Dunfallandy example it is hard to resist the conclusion that this was one of many scenes drawn either from a compilation of strange animals or perhaps from folklore.

There are, however, three other subjects which are dealt with more fully and more convincingly in Pictish sculpture. These are the stories of Daniel and David as given in the Old Testament and the incident recounted by the early fathers of the meeting of the hermits Paul and Anthony in Egypt. It is noticeable that, among the early Christians, certain key incidents were remembered concerning Old Testament characters. There was a preference for 'salvation' themes which foreshadowed the salvation for all men brought by Christ. Thus Daniel, through his faith in God, was saved from the lions' den, while David saved the sheep from the lion, whose jaws he rent with his bare hands.

Daniel was a favourite subject from the beginning of early Christian art. The posture of Daniel and the number of lions included varies considerably. The back of a cross-slab at Meigle in Tayside (figure 16) shows Daniel in a priest-like attitude with two lions on each side. He is placed centrally on the slab and dominates the total composition: indeed, it may be that the sculptor was expressing God's dominance over the whole animal kingdom, for above the figure of Daniel are several horsemen and below him a centaur and a dragon seizing a horned beast. A closely similar representation of Daniel may be seen in the centre of the east face of the Market Cross at Kells in Ireland and Daniel appears on many other Irish crosses.

The full development of the 'boss' style noted on the cross-slab at Dunfallandy may be seen on the magnificent cross-slab at Nigg in Easter Ross, Highland, and nearby at Shandwick, where a slab with a cross composed entirely of boss ornament is situated on

17. Top of cross-slab, Nigg, Easter Ross, Highland. (Photograph: Royal Commission on Ancient Monuments, Scotland.)

rising ground overlooking the Moray Firth. The slab at Nigg is now housed in the church there and has been restored to its full height following earlier damage. At the top of this slab is a skilfully carved scene from the story of the hermits Paul and Anthony in the desert (figure 17). Jerome tells how a raven, which usually brought Paul half a loaf of bread, brought a whole loaf when Anthony visited him. Usually the scene is shown with Paul and Anthony seated facing each other with a round loaf of bread between them. It has been suggested that, in the Nigg representation, Paul and Anthony are shown kneeling because of the restricted space available to the sculptor. However, their kneeling attitude, the fact that they are holding books and the representation of the raven, which is about to place the bread on a ceremonial plate or chalice, suggest that the scene has been transformed into a celebration of the Mass. This scene may therefore represent a development in the doctrine of the eucharist and of the liturgical practices associated with it. (The animals in the foreground probably represent the lions which, in the traditional story, helped Anthony to bury Paul.)

Scenes from the life of David are shown on a number of Pictish slabs. The most complete David cycle is carved on what is generally regarded as the high point of Pictish art, one of the panels of a stone coffin or shrine, now in the museum at St Andrews Cathedral in Fife (figure 18). Here David is shown in bold relief (on the right) rending the lion's jaw, while in the centre a smaller figure of David on horseback is shown defending the sheep from a lion. The figure below may also represent David as a warrior. This high-relief sculpture has been compared with Mercian examples and with the Anglian cross at Ruthwell, and is thought to date from the late eighth or early ninth century.

With the high-relief carving at St Andrews we reach the ninth century and Romilly Allen's Class III stones which were devoid of Pictish symbols. This was not the end of Pictish influence on sculpture, but it diminished, especially after the union with the Scots in 843. Romilly Allen's Class III stones are a very miscellaneous group. He includes, for example, the crosses erected in southern Scotland during the Northumbrian occupation and the Whithorn school of sculpture of the tenth and eleventh centuries, which was influenced by Irish-Norse connections and produced disc-headed crosses comparable with late crosses in Wales and Cornwall. A number of Norse cross-slabs are also included from this late period, as well as the earlier high crosses of Iona, described in chapter 4.

Cross-slabs continued to be carved in Scotland from the ninth century onwards and recumbent monuments known as hogbacks also made their appearance in the tenth and eleventh centuries. (There is an important collection of these in the old parish church at Govan, Glasgow, which contains one of the most interesting

18. Panel of shrine, St Andrews, Fife. (Photograph: Royal Commission on Ancient Monuments, Scotland.)

but least known collections of early Christian stones in Scotland.) The outstanding quality of the Pictish cross-slabs has tended to distract attention from the free-standing crosses which began to be erected under Irish influence from the ninth century onwards. These survive not only in western Scotland, as at Kilmartin, Keills, Barochan (now moved to Paisley Abbey) and Hamilton, all in Strathclyde, but also in eastern Scotland, as at Dupplin (near Forteviot, Tayside) and Camustone (near Monikie, Tayside). The tallest of all the monuments of this period in Scotland is 'Sueno's Stone' at Forres in Grampian, standing over 20 feet (6 metres) high and carved from a single slab of sandstone. The extraordinary rows of warriors carved on the back of this slab have attracted the most attention but the ringed cross with extended shaft on the front reminds us that this, too, was a cross-slab.

Turning now to the Isle of Man during this period, we find that the rough cross-decorated stones described in chapter 1 developed into shaped and sculptured cross-slabs, as was also happening in Wales and Ireland. In the Isle of Man Kermode divided the early Christian monuments into two classes: I, Pre-Scandinavian; and II, Scandinavian. Viking raids on the Isle of Man began in 798 and Viking settlement on the island increased rapidly during the following two centuries. Kermode points out, however, that nearly two-thirds of the total number of surviving monuments pre-date the main Viking settlement and that there was continuity between the Celtic and later Scandinavian crosses, particularly in the continued use of the ringed form. The crosses carved by the Vikings after they had adopted the Christian religion of the Celtic inhabitants have been widely admired, but the pre-Scandinavian crosses are our main concern here and they also show considerable skill and artistry. A ninth-century slab from Maughold with a Celtic ring-headed cross in low relief (and also a Manx version of the meeting of Paul and Anthony) is illustrated (figure 19). Maughold was the main centre of pre-Viking Christianity in the island but almost every parish still has remains of ecclesiastical settlements or 'keeills', which probably began in the pre-Viking period and were further established after the Norsemen adopted Christianity. Celtic sculptors also developed disc-headed cross-slabs, of which there is a particularly attractive example at Lonan (figure 20). This is probably in its original position near the old church and, though of ninth-century or even tenth-century date, it shows Celtic rather than Norse decoration.

19. (Left) Cross-slab, Maughold, Isle of Man. (Photograph: Manx Museum and National Trust.)

20. (Right) Cross-slab, Lonan, Isle of Man. (Photograph: Manx Museum and National Trust.)

The most notable example of Celtic sculpture in the Isle of Man dates from the late eighth century. This is the Crucifixion scene from what may have been an altar-frontal found in the ruins of an early Christian chapel on the Calf of Man, the small island off the south-west coast now owned by the National Trust. This stone (illustrated in figure 21) is now in the Manx Museum at Douglas. It shows Christ dressed in an elaborate robe. The open eyes indicate that Christ is still alive, and the figure of the lance-bearer on the left would have been matched by a similar figure of the sponge-bearer on the right. The circular ornamental feature in the centre of Christ's body suggests that the artist was working from a metal prototype and this representation is often compared

21. The Calf of Man Crucifixion, now in the Manx Museum, Douglas. (Photograph: Manx Museum and National Trust.)

with an eighth-century bronze plaque which had probably been riveted to a book cover from Athlone in Ireland. Byzantine influence has been noted in contemporary manuscript work and the Calf of Man Crucifixion shows the bearded and robed Christ of the eastern tradition rather than the clean-shaven, semi-naked Christ of the western tradition found earlier in Ireland.

3
Sculptured crosses
of Wales and Cornwall

In Wales and Cornwall the period from the fifth to the ninth centuries, when Christianity was establishing itself, produced the inscribed and cross-decorated stones described in chapter 1. There is little in the sculpture of Wales and Cornwall during the eighth century to compare with the Pictish cross-slabs, but there was a great variety of cross-decorated stones and it was from these that sculptured cross-slabs seem to have emerged by a process of gradual evolution. In Wales, regular forms of cross-slab had developed by the ninth and tenth centuries, as well as free-standing crosses. In Cornwall, there is a gap between the inscribed stones of the fifth, sixth and seventh centuries and the beginning of free-standing crosses in the ninth and tenth centuries. The Saxons had advanced to Cornwall by the ninth century and Aethelstan received the submission of the king of Cornwall in 926, but in Wales the construction of Offa's Dyke in the eighth century established a *modus vivendi* which lasted until the Norman conquest. The sculpture of Wales was considerably influenced by English and Irish forms of decoration, however. Towards the end of this period the influence of Anglo-Viking art may also be detected.

Nash-Williams noted 125 sculptured monuments in Wales (his Group III) and several more have been discovered since his list was published in 1950. Nearly half of this group occur in Glamorgan, which was most open to cultural influences from the east. There are also notable concentrations in Pembrokeshire (western Dyfed) and Anglesey, which were both open to Irish influences. The distribution of the stones indicates that there were schools of sculptors at Penmon in Anglesey (Gwynedd), St Davids in Dyfed and at Margam, Merthyr Mawr and Llantwit Major in Glamorgan. This, in itself, is important evidence of the development of ecclesiastical centres in Wales.

The transition from incised to sculptured work in relief and the shaping of the stones into more regular forms may be illustrated from the small pillar-stone (2 feet or 0.6 metres high) from Tregaron in Dyfed, now in the National Museum of Wales (see figure 22). Here the cross, the form of which is derived from the chi-rho, is made to stand out from the stone by the simple device of carving away the quadrants of the circle and the 'spike' is

22. (Left) 'Enevir' pillar-stone, Tregaron, Dyfed, now in the National Museum of Wales.
23. (Right) 'Ilquici' cross-slab, Margam, West Glamorgan, now in the Margam Abbey museum. (Photograph: National Monuments Record, Wales.)

faintly visible below the circle. The inscription on the side of the stone to someone called Enevir is in the half-uncial form of lettering which developed from the Roman capitals used on the earlier monuments, and this stone is dated to the period from the seventh to the ninth century partly for that reason. This type of memorial stone developed into taller and wider cross-slabs, comparable in size to those in Pictland and the Isle of Man and often intricately carved in relief. In Glamorgan, an unusual form known as the 'panelled' or 'cartwheel' slab emerged in the late ninth century and continued into the tenth and eleventh centuries. The largest example of this type, standing nearly 7 feet (1.93 metres) high, may be seen in the Margam Abbey museum (figure 23). The head is filled with a large ring-cross carved in

24. (Left) 'Conbelin' cross-slab, Margam, West Glamorgan, now in the Margam Abbey museum. (Photograph: National Museum of Wales.)
25. (Right) 'Houelt' slab-cross, Llantwit Major, South Glamorgan.

relief, and the Latin inscription below, now badly worn, is thought to read 'This is the stone of Ilquici'. It belongs to the final phase of the early Christian period in South Wales.

The most distinctive form of the cross-slab developed in South Wales was the so-called 'disc-headed' type, comparable with those which are found in the Isle of Man. The finest of them, which again may be seen in the Margam museum, is the famous 'Conbelin' stone, which is dated to the late ninth or early tenth century (see figure 24). It consists of a relatively thin slab of the local Pennant sandstone with a disc 42 inches (1.1 metres) in diameter and carved with a double-square angled cross of the type noted on some of the Pictish slabs. The shaft may originally have been as tall as the head and is carved with two figures which probably represent St John (on the left, a bearded figure holding a book) and the Virgin Mary (on the right, with a collared robe). These biblical figures were sometimes shown at the foot of the cross in early Christian art, either in place of, or in addition to, the lance-bearer and sponge-bearer.

The disc-head with a short shaft, as at Margam and elsewhere in that area, may be compared with the disc-headed slabs with longer shafts, of which the best example is in the church at Llantwit Major (see figure 25). The Latin inscription carved at the base of the shaft reads in translation: 'In the name of God, the Father, and the Holy Spirit, Houelt prepared this cross for the soul of Res his father.' The name Houelt is probably a reference to Hywel ap Rhys, a local king who died in 886, and this is one of the very few sculptured stones of the period which can be dated with accuracy. It may be noted that, although the form of this monument may appear to be a development of the Conbelin stone, it is of a similar date. The Houelt stone also raises the question: at what point does a cross-slab become a free-standing cross? The Royal Commission on Ancient and Historical Monuments in Wales classifies it as a 'disc-headed slab', while Nash-Williams calls it a 'slab-cross'. It is clear that cross-slabs and free-standing crosses developed side by side in Wales and Ireland, and one cannot assume that one developed from the other. It may nevertheless be worth noting that free-standing crosses (particularly in South Wales) were often 'composite', that is made up of several pieces, with the cross-head carved separately from the shaft. From one point of view, some of these composite crosses may be regarded as elongated slabs surmounted with a cross.

There is one other disc-headed cross-slab of the Margam type which is worthy of special comment. This may be seen in the churchyard at Llangan, in South Glamorgan, protected by a modern shelter (figure 26). This slab, though badly worn, is of particular interest because it has one of the rare representations of the Crucifixion on a Welsh monument of this period (late ninth or early tenth century). There are the usual figures of the lance-bearer and sponge-bearer on each side of the cross and Christ is shown dressed only in a loin cloth, as on the incised slab at Inishkea North (figure 11). Below the cross is a very worn figure with extended arms, holding in the right hand a small cylindrical object and in the left an inward-curving horn or bow. This could be Mary Magdalene holding a phial of ointment (as on the Gosforth cross in Cumbria) or the figure could be male,

26. Disc-headed cross-slab, Llangan, South Glamorgan.

perhaps David or St Peter. In any event the inspiration was probably Irish.

So far the cross-slabs described have been in South Wales, where indeed they are most plentiful. Those in North and Central Wales are fewer in number but of considerable interest. A tall slab with a wheel-cross of Celtic type now stands inside the church at Llanrhaiadr-ym-Mochnant in Clwyd (figure 27). Nash-Williams dated this to the ninth or tenth century, other scholars to the eleventh. It has plaited interlace to the left of the shaft, fret-pattern on the right, and spirals in the spandrels at the top, all drawn from the usual repertoire of sculptured decoration of the period. Across the arm of the cross is a Latin inscription with an abbreviated name which cannot now be deciphered with certainty but may refer to a Welsh ruler called Gwgan who died in the eleventh century. The inscription is preceded by a small, equal-armed cross, which is a similar formula to that used on some of the slabs in Pembrokeshire which were inscribed CRUX XPI, the Cross of Christ.

Almost certainly of eleventh-century date is the noble cross-slab which now stands inside the church at Llowes in Powys (figure 28). This slab is decorated on the front with a large wheel-cross carved in high relief and filled with diamond-shaped patterns in lower relief. Like some of the earlier Pictish slabs, this has the architectural presence of a free-standing cross, though of the Irish type (see chapter 4). Also in Powys, in the church at Meifod, is another notable cross-slab. It tapers in width, suggesting that it is the lid of a stone coffin, and Nash-Williams considered it to have been copied from Merovingian examples of the eighth century to be found in France, although this has been disputed. However, the crucifix ring-cross, the Celtic plaits and the Viking knots and animals are of great interest (figure 29). The

27. (Left) Cross-slab, Llanrhaiadr-ym-Mochnant, Clwyd.
28. (Right) Cross-slab, Llowes, Powys. (Photograph: Mike Seaborne.)

29. Upper part of cross-slab, Meifod, Powys.

Crucifixion shows Christ wearing a loincloth, as at Llangan, and nail holes are visible in the hands and feet. The ornamentation may have a symbolic significance, with the triquetra (three interlaced arcs) and other knots representing Christian beliefs dominating the snakes and a very fearsome rodent representing the forces of evil.

Turning now to the free-standing crosses in Wales, there are two relatively small but elegant examples of monolithic crosses at Laugharne in Dyfed and from Llanynys in Powys, both dating

30. (Left) 'Neuadd Siarman' cross, Llanynys, Powys, now in the Brecknock Museum.
31. (Right) Cast of the 'Irbic' cross, National Museum of Wales.

from the late ninth or early tenth century. The latter, known as the 'Neuadd Siarman' cross, is 6 feet (1.8 metres) high and is now in the Brecknock Museum (figure 30). The most distinctive feature of this cross is the moulding on the edges of the shaft, comparable with examples in southern England, as at Codford St Peter in Wiltshire. The knotwork and interlace are very competently carved and this cross is generally regarded as one of the finest in Wales. Similar angle-moulding is carried to excess in the later composite cross which stands (without its head) in the churchyard at Llandough in South Glamorgan. The National Museum of Wales has a cast of this cross, a photograph of which appears as figure 31. As an experiment, the cast has been painted, since there is evidence on other pieces of sculpture of this period that monuments of this type were originally painted. This has made it possible to pick out more clearly the horseman and the bust of a man carved on the sides of the rectangular base. There is also an inscription to an otherwise unknown person called Irbic. This cross is dated to the late tenth or eleventh century.

There are three other notable free-standing crosses in South Wales, again dating from late in the period, and all in Pembrokeshire. The earliest of these stands inside the church at Penally and dates from the first half of the tenth century. The shaft has vine-scroll decoration of Northumbrian type, while a fragment of another cross-shaft kept inside the church has confronted animals of the 'Anglian beast' type, again showing English influence. Two more famous tall crosses in Pembrokeshire are the Carew cross, which stands in a walled enclosure at the roadside adjacent to Carew Castle, and the cross in the churchyard at Nevern, south-west of Cardigan, illustrated in figure 32. They are both of similar form, about 13 feet (4 metres) in height, and are of composite construction, with the cross-heads attached to the shafts by tenon joints. The decoration of the shafts is of the Celtic type but shows some Scandinavian influence and is arranged in square or oblong panels. The Carew cross has an inscription to Maredudd ap Edwin, who ruled that part of Wales from 1033 to 1035, so this is a royal memorial, like the Houelt stone at Llantwit Major. There are two inscriptions on the Nevern cross: the meaning of the one on the front is not known, while the one on the back has the letters DNS, for *Dominus* (Lord). These two crosses, to judge from their similarity of style, are contemporary with each other.

In North Wales there are two large crosses at Penmon Priory in Anglesey and one near Whitford in Clwyd, which is generally known as 'Maen Achwyfan'. They all date from the late tenth or early eleventh century and are of Anglo-Viking character. During this period Scandinavian influence from the Norse settlements in Ireland and the Isle of Man extended along the coasts of North Wales, Lancashire and Cumbria, where other crosses with Viking characteristics survive, notably at Halton near Lancaster and Gosforth in Cumbria. The two crosses at Penmon, which are now kept in the later priory buildings, have disc-heads (both unfortunately damaged) with projections or 'ears'. These are similar to the cross-heads which may still be seen in St John's church in

Chester, where there was an important Viking settlement and an established school of sculptors.

The best preserved of the North Wales crosses is Maen Achwyfan, which stands in what is thought to be its original position in a field about a mile (1.6 km) west of the village of Whitford and is illustrated in figure 33. It is of monolithic construction and is 11 feet (3.4 metres) high. It also has a circular head of the Chester type, but without the 'ears', and there is ring-chain ornament on the side of the shaft characteristic of Norse sculpture of this period. One of the crosses at Penmon has a carving on its shaft of the hermit Anthony tempted by animal-headed devils, a further episode in the story of Paul and Anthony which was noted on some of the Pictish slabs and which also occurs in Ireland (chapter 4). This Christian motif contrasts with the figure of a man on the shaft of the Whitford cross, whose stance is thought to be in the pre-Christian tradition of cult figures with fertility overtones.

External influences are also apparent in the case of the famous 'Pillar of Eliseg' near Llangollen in Clwyd, which is part of the shaft of a cross, the head of which is also lost. It bore an inscription which is now worn away but was transcribed in 1696. This stated that the cross was erected by Cyngen, the last of the kings of Powys, in honour of his great-grandfather, Eliseg. Cyngen died in 854, after which Powys passed to the kings of Gwynedd. The round shaft of this pillar-cross is characteristic of Mercian crosses carved during this period and three similar shafts (no longer *in situ*) may be seen in the West Park at Macclesfield, Cheshire. The pillar of Eliseg is chiefly worth visiting because of its historical associations and its beautiful siting close to the later Cistercian abbey of Valle Crucis, but the only inscription now visible on it is one to T. Lloyd, who re-erected the broken shaft in 1779.

Throughout this period Cornwall was closely linked to South Wales. Cornwall has more crosses than any other county but it is now recognised that the very great majority of them date from the late eleventh, twelfth and early thirteenth centuries, that is outside the early Christian period which is the subject of this book. Even so, it is clear that this later practice of erecting free-standing crosses in churchyards and small wayside crosses marking the paths leading to parish churches (which, it has been convincingly argued, was a by-product of the development of a parochial system in the post-Norman period) may well have developed from an earlier tradition of stone crosses. Langdon's

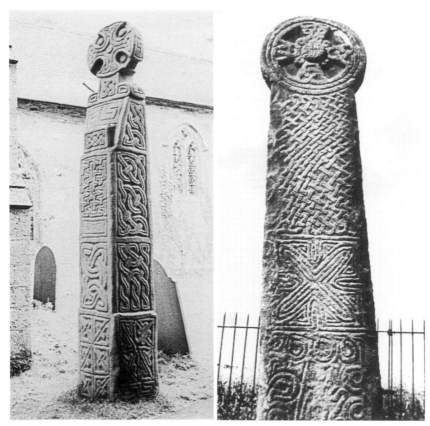

32. (Left) Composite pillar-cross, Nevern, Dyfed. (Photograph: National Monuments Record, Wales.)
33. (Right) 'Maen Achwyfan' cross, Whitford, Clwyd.

study, *Old Cornish Crosses* (1896), divided his 360 examples into Class A (unornamented crosses), Class B (ornamented crosses) and Class C (miscellaneous monuments). This last group includes only five early cross-slabs and, though there were probably more, the gap between the numerous early inscribed stones of Cornwall and the later free-standing crosses is difficult to bridge.

Professor Charles Thomas has provided important clues to the origin of the later Cornish crosses by pointing to the monastery of St Buryan near Land's End and that of St Petroc at Bodmin, both of which flourished in the tenth century. These centres could well

34. (Left) Cross at Cardinham, Cornwall. (Photograph: Royal Institution of Cornwall.)
35. (Right) Cross at Lanherne, Cornwall. (Photograph: Royal Institution of Cornwall.)

36. Cross at Perranporth, Cornwall. (Photograph: Royal Institution of Cornwall.)

have had schools of sculptors attached to them, as was probably the case with some of the monasteries in South Wales. It is also significant that some of the earliest and most skilfully carved of the free-standing crosses are in the Bodmin and Land's End areas of Cornwall.

First there is part of a cross-shaft which stands about a mile (1.6 km) north-west of St Cleer near the main road to Liskeard. This is known as the 'Doniert' stone after an inscription on it which names Doniert, who is also mentioned in an early Welsh source as the king of Cornwall in about 875. North-east of Bodmin, in the churchyard of Cardinham, is a fine wheel-headed cross with the most southerly example known of Scandinavian-style ring-chain ornament. This cross, which is illustrated in figure 34, is dated on stylistic grounds to the tenth century.

At Sancreed, the parish next to St Buryan, there are two crosses in the churchyard, both with wheel-heads and the robed figure of the crucified Christ carved on them. The cross near the south porch has interlace work of tenth-century type and also has inscribed on it the name Runhol, which may be assumed to be that of the sculptor, especially as the same name appears on the back of a similar cross formerly in the nearby parish of Gwinear, from where it was moved to Lanherne, where it now stands near the chapel door of Lanherne convent (see figure 35). The robed figure of Christ also appears on several diminutive crosses in St Buryan parish, the earliest of which, as noted earlier, could have been the model used by Runhol for the heads of his much taller crosses.

Certainly, crosses with circular heads of various forms later became fully established in Cornwall. At Perranporth, near the 'lost church' of St Piran which was buried in the sand-dunes, stands a cross (illustrated in figure 36) which is mentioned in a charter of 960 and is one of the very few in Cornwall which can be credited with an early date. It may be argued that the hard local granite did not make fine decoration easy (as was also the case with the Wicklow granite used for some of the Irish crosses). The later crosses of Cornwall, though frequently plain and difficult to date, have nevertheless a quiet dignity which is often enhanced by the remoteness of the places where they were erected.

4
High crosses of Iona and Ireland

For the ring-headed stone cross in its most developed form one looks to Ireland and Iona. There has been much discussion about the origin of the 'high' free-standing cross. There are many free-armed Anglian examples (that is, without the ring-head) reaching a superb climax with the Ruthwell cross in Dumfries-shire, which is usually dated to the eighth century. The iconography of the Ruthwell cross also broke new ground. Apart from the sharing of bread between the hermits Paul and Anthony, all the scenes represented on the Ruthwell cross came from the life of Christ. The front of the cross is dominated by a magnificent carving of Christ in Majesty, while the Crucifixion is at the bottom of the opposite side. The position occupied by the Crucifixion and the absence of Old Testament scenes contrast markedly with the development of Christian iconography on the later Irish crosses.

W. G. Collingwood, who published the first major study of Northumbrian crosses in 1927, believed that the first tall crosses were rood-staffs, carved in wood and later imitated in stone. Among later crosses, the Anglo-Viking cross at Gosforth in Cumbria, with its rounded shaft and graceful form, gives the clearest impression of a wooden prototype. It is nevertheless possible that, in places where suitable stone was available and a local tradition of building in stone persisted, crosses of consider-able height could have been originally conceived in stone, as seems to have happened with several of the Welsh crosses already considered.

Dr Françoise Henry, who studied the Irish crosses over many years, pointed to a number of stone slabs which she considered to be of seventh-century date, where the crosses seem to be trying to 'escape' from the slabs on which they were carved. She cites, for example, the cross-slab which now stands behind St Kevin's church on the beautiful early monastic site at Glendalough in County Wicklow (figure 37). Here the cross takes up the whole of the available space and the slab is shaped into a projection at the top. There is a similar example at Fahan, further north in County Donegal, where there are projections on both sides of the slab. We noted on a number of cross-slabs in Pictland and Wales the architectural effect achieved when the crosses were carved to stand out from the background. The same effect may be seen on the slab excavated at Gallen Priory in County Offaly (see figure

37. (Left) Cross-slab, Glendalough, Wicklow.
38. (Right) Cross-slab, Gallen, County Offaly. (Photograph: National Museum of Ireland.)

38). This is also related to the 'face cross' group of stones, which have been noted in other parts of Ireland and in Scotland, where there is a particularly fine example at Kiloran on Colonsay (the Riasg Buidhe cross). This type of cross is thought to have originated in Coptic Egypt and, as Professor Thomas has noted, these crosses with encircled faces closely resemble the (usually later) representations of the crucified Christ.

The first of the free-standing stone crosses in Ireland, considered by Dr Henry to illustrate the final 'escape' of the cross from its slab, is the remarkable cross at Carndonagh, also in County Donegal (figure 39). It is about 10 feet (3 metres) high and is carved from one thin sandstone slab. The cross-form is composed of a broad ribbon forming a continuous decoration, and below it there is a front-facing figure which Dr Henry considered to be Christ in Glory, but which a later authority considers to be the Crucifixion. Placed on each side of the cross are two small pillars, one with a man's head emerging from the mouth of a fish (probably Jonah) and the other with a warrior who may represent David.

The cross at Carndonagh may have 'escaped' from the slab, but the ring had also disappeared. It has, indeed, been argued that the Fahan and Carndonagh crosses were a purely regional development, unrelated to the development of the high, ringed cross. It was the achievement of sculptors in other parts of Ireland and in Iona to use the ring not only as a decorative device but also

39. Cross at Carndonagh, County Donegal. (Photograph: Commissioners of Public Works, Ireland.)

to perform the functional purpose of supporting the arms. This made it possible to change the shape of the head of the cross and to create further surfaces which could be ornamented. The development of the stone ring joining the arms of free-standing crosses belongs to the eighth century, and with it came the dividing up of the shaft and arms into panels containing interlace and other decorative motifs and, as time went on, a growing number of scriptural subjects until they dominated the whole cross.

The earliest of the free-standing ringed crosses in Ireland are usually considered to be those at Ahenny in County Tipperary, which some authorities date as early as 700 and others to later in the eighth century. It is often suggested that the prototypes of the North and South Crosses at Ahenny, which are 12 and 11 feet (3.6 and 3.3 metres) high respectively, may have been wooden crosses of similar form. Certainly it is interesting that on the base of the North Cross there is a carving of a figure holding a ring-headed processional cross, presumably of wood. It has also been suggested that the elaborate decoration of these crosses may have been in imitation of wooden crosses with decorative sheets of bronze nailed to them. It is equally possible, however, that the bosses and other 'metalwork' features were directly imitated from portable metal objects, as is thought to have been the case with the Calf of Man sculpture mentioned in chapter 2. The front, back and sides of the Ahenny crosses are beautifully carved with interlace and spiral work (see figure 40). It may be noted that figure work, with processions of men and animals similar to those on some of the Pictish slabs and no doubt ultimately derived from classical sources, was confined to the base of each cross, a position favoured for non-biblical subjects on some of the later high crosses in Ireland.

The eighth-century crosses at Iona and Kildalton are justly famous and are most appropriately mentioned in an Irish context because of the close links which existed during that period between Iona and Ireland. Iona occupied a key position between Pictland and Northumbria on the one hand and Ireland on the other, and it has often been pointed out that this was the meeting point of different artistic traditions, which were expressed not only in sculpture but also in illuminated manuscripts, notably the Book of Kells. The crosses at Iona were reappraised by the Royal Commission on the Ancient and Historical Monuments of Scotland in 1982. The Commissioners considered that St John's, St Martin's and St Oran's Crosses were probably carved in the

40. (Left) South Cross, Ahenny, County Tipperary. (Photograph: Commissioners of Public Works, Ireland.)
41. (Right) St Martin's Cross, Iona, Strathclyde. (Photograph: Royal Commission on Ancient Monuments, Scotland.)

second half of the eighth century, while the surviving shaft of St Matthew's Cross probably dates from the late ninth or tenth century. (Maclean's Cross, which stands further away from the abbey, near the parish church, is a product of the later Iona school and is of fifteenth-century date.)

Of the major crosses which originally stood on the site of the early monastery at Iona, St Oran's survives only in fragments (now in the Nunnery Museum nearby). St John's Cross was also

in a fragmentary condition and is undergoing repair. A replica of
the complete cross now stands on the original base. It is thought
that St John's Cross, which had the widest span of any early cross
in Britain, was originally without a ring and that, owing to
structural weakness, the quadrants were fitted in later. The most
perfect of the surviving crosses is that of St Martin, which is
shown in figure 41. Its height, including the base, is nearly 17 feet
(5.1 metres) and there are slots in the ends of the arms which may
have housed wooden extensions or metalwork decoration, which
would have changed the proportions of the cross as we now see it.
The proportions are in any event markedly different from those
of the Ahenny crosses. The west face has a carving of the Virgin
and Child supported by angels (similar to the representation of
the Virgin in the Book of Kells), with Daniel in the lions' den,
Abraham's sacrifice of Isaac, and David with musicians on the
shaft below. The east face, shown here, is decorated with
serpent-and-boss ornament carved with great skill. It may be
noted that the stone used for this cross came from mid Argyll and
some writers have suggested that the sculptor may have come
from Pictland, where boss work was well developed, as at Nigg
and Shandwick. Other writers have pointed out the similarity of
the decorative work to that on the South Cross at Clonmacnois in
County Offaly, considered below.

The most famous cross of the Iona school, and the most perfect
surviving example of a ringed cross in Scotland, is to be found in
the churchyard at Kildalton on the island of Islay. The head and
shaft of this beautiful cross are carved with consummate skill
from a single block of stone nearly 9 feet (2.7 metres) high. On
the east face there is a similar representation of the Virgin and
Child to that on St Martin's Cross at Iona, but here it is not in the
centre of the cross-head but on the shaft immediately below (see
figure 42). On the arms of the cross are scenes usually identified
as Cain's murder of Abel (left), David fighting the lion (top) and
Abraham's sacrifice of Isaac (right). The west face has serpent-
and-boss work closely comparable with St Martin's Cross but with
the addition of four animals in high relief, surrounding the central
boss.

We now turn to the high crosses of Ireland, where, it may be
argued, the art of the sculptured cross reached its highest point of
development. Between sixty and seventy examples have survived
in the centre and north of Ireland, often in their original locations
on early monastic sites. As with the crosses at Iona, the settings of
the Irish crosses add greatly to their interest, and again there are

42. Cross at Kildalton, Islay, Strathclyde. (Photograph: Royal Commission on Ancient Monuments, Scotland.)

usually several crosses on each major monastic site. These crosses were intended to mark out the precinct of the monastery and were not designed to act primarily as individual memorials: their purpose was didactic, illustrating the way that God protected the people of Israel and the salvation brought to all men by Jesus. We will find that the emphasis given to the Virgin and Child on the crosses at Iona and Kildalton was not continued on the Irish crosses. Instead, representations of the Crucifixion of Christ increase in prominence and are invariably on the west faces of the crosses. The east faces gradually come to be occupied by representations of the Risen Lord. Scenes from the Passion and Crucifixion become more detailed and are balanced by scenes showing Christ's resurrection and final triumph. A similar balance between Old and New Testament scenes also emerges.

As with most of the sculpture of this period, exact dating is impossible, apart from a small number of crosses which carry inscriptions, and these, too, are often difficult to interpret. However, it is clear that there was a great surge forward in the late eighth and early ninth centuries, and a further major advance in the early tenth century. In view of the large number of surviving high crosses in Ireland it is necessary to be selective and to concentrate on five major sites, all within daily travelling distance of Dublin.

We begin with the former monastic sites at Moone and Castledermot in County Kildare, where the crosses have all been dated to the late eighth or early ninth centuries. Only one complete cross has survived at Moone but it is perhaps the most striking of all the high crosses in Ireland. It is 17 feet (5.1 metres) high and is constructed from several blocks of the local Wicklow granite (figure 43). As at Ahenny, the figural scenes are on the base, but here they extend to a transitional stone between the base and the shaft, and there is also a carving of the Risen Christ at the top of the east side of the shaft. On the west side, illustrated here, the transitional stone has a relatively small representation of the Crucifixion with the usual lance-bearer and sponge-bearer. Below this is a remarkable panel of the twelve apostles, with squares indicating their bodies and arms (they decrease in size from the bottom row upwards). It has been suggested that the hard local granite used for this cross may have made carving more naturalistic figures impossible, and these and the other figures are often described as naive. It is more likely that the form of the figures was intentionally contrived. Analogies may be found with square-bodied figures enamelled

43. (Left) Cross at Moone, County Kildare.
44. (Above) Detail of cross at Moone: Paul and Anthony; the Temptation of Anthony.

on eighth-century bowls, and it is probable that the non-naturalistic character of the figure work on the Moone cross was a decorative device, perhaps influenced by the desire to avoid any suggestion of idolatry. (In the Byzantine church between 730 and 843 the depiction of figural subjects was banned for that reason.) The north side of the base has scenes from the story of the hermits Paul and Anthony (figure 44) while the south side has the Old Testament story of the children of Israel in the fiery furnace and the New Testament accounts of the flight of Mary and Joseph into Egypt and the miracle of the loaves and fishes. The east side shows Adam and Eve, the sacrifice of Isaac and Daniel in the lions' den.

It is possible to see logical connections between the scenes
shown on the cross at Moone, but the scenes represented on the
two crosses nearby at Castledermot, again carved from Wicklow
granite, seem to be arranged in more arbitrary fashion. The
figures, particularly on the North Cross, are even more doll-like
than at Moone. On the west face of the North Cross a Crucifixion
scene of oriental type occupies the most prominent place in the
centre of the head and the corresponding position on the east face
shows the Fall of Man, with Eve handing the apple to Adam. The
South Cross, shown in figure 45, is better preserved and has
figure work only on the west face and on the sides and base, the
east face being wholly occupied by interlace patterns. On the west
face shown here the Crucifixion is in the centre of the head, with
four panels below showing Paul and Anthony sharing the bread,
Adam and Eve sharing the apple, the temptation of Anthony by
animal-headed devils, and Daniel in the lions' den. There is an
artistic link between these scenes (the bread and apple in the first
two scenes and the men flanked by animals in the third and fourth
scenes) but the theological message is less coherent. On the base
of this cross is a scene showing two men with spears hunting
several different kinds of animal and a bird, or this scene could
represent the animals being driven into the ark.

We now move northwards to the site of the important
monastery at Kells in County Meath. Here there are four crosses,
three of them in the churchyard and one standing amid the traffic
in the market place nearby. The largest cross in the churchyard,
known as the Unfinished Cross, is considerably later in date than
the others (eleventh or twelfth century) but is of interest as it
shows some of the stages involved in carving a major stone cross.
It should be noted, however, that this cross was assembled in
modern times from the loose pieces which had survived, and it is
unlikely that the sculptor would have worked on the cross in its
present upright position. The other crosses at Kells date from the
late eighth or early ninth century. The second cross to be seen in
the churchyard is known as the Broken Cross and consists only of
part of a shaft. Despite its incomplete and worn condition, it is
well worth studying for the interesting scenes depicted, including
one showing the baptism of Christ (figure 46). The river Jordan is
indicated by two streams of water issuing from circular objects
which are thought to represent the urns held by the personified
Father Jordan in late classical representations of the baptism of
Christ and also shown in Carolingian art of this period. On this
panel John is baptising a diminutive Christ with a baptismal

45. South Cross, Castledermot, County Kildare.

spoon and the dove is shown descending, feet first. On the further shore are two onlookers wearing long robes.

The most complete of the crosses in the churchyard at Kells, though also very worn, is the South Cross by the round tower. The style of carving on this cross has been compared with

manuscript work, since the panels are loosely arranged in a
manner more reminiscent of the scribe or embroiderer than the
worker in stone. In the panel showing Adam and Eve on the left
and Cain and Abel on the right (figure 47), the figures have been
aptly described as 'dancing' on the stone. The cross itself, like the
one in the market place, shows a great variety of subjects. This
was clearly a period when the sources for Christian iconography
were more varied than ever before and included subjects
rediscovered or invented during the renaissance in Carolingian
art which was taking place during this period.

A closer examination of the decoration of the South Cross and
of the Market Cross reveals indications that the sculptors may to
some extent have been overwhelmed by the richness of the
repertoire of images from which they could draw. On the South
Cross by the tower the centre of the west face is taken up by a
new image of Christ in Glory, holding a cross and flowering
bough in the so-called Osirian attitude of one of the figures in the
Book of Kells. This displaces the Crucifixion, which appears
immediately below. Having, therefore, employed the two prin-
cipal images of the Crucified and Risen Lord, the east face has no
figure at all in the centre of the head but a circle filled with small

46. Detail of the Broken Cross, Kells, County Meath: the Baptism of Christ.

47. (Left) Detail of South Cross, Kells, County Meath: Adam and Eve; Cain and Abel.
48. (Right) South Cross, Clonmacnois, County Offaly. (Photograph: Commissioners of Public Works, Ireland.)

bosses. The rest of the space is taken up with Old Testament scenes. On the Market Cross, the centre of the head of the west face is occupied by the Crucifixion and the shaft by a number of New Testament scenes, while on the east face the centre of the head is filled with a Christ-like representation of Daniel in the lions' den, with a mixture of Old and New Testament scenes on the shaft below.

Most of these tensions were to be resolved a century later on the Cross of the Scriptures at Clonmacnois and on the two crosses which survive at Monasterboice, all of which date from the early tenth century. Clonmacnois is perhaps the finest of all the monastic sites in Ireland, beautifully situated on the river Shannon in County Offaly. At the entrance to the site is a small courtyard with a series of carved recumbent slabs, for which Clonmacnois was well known, now mounted upright on the walls. The site itself is full of modern 'Celtic' crosses but there is no difficulty in recognising the crosses of the early Christian period. The oldest of these (dated to about 800), which survives as a shaft

49. Cross of the Scriptures, Clonmacnois, County Offaly.

without its head to the North of the ruins of the former cathedral, is interesting as it includes a carving of the cross-legged Celtic god Cernunnos. This reminds us that, as with one of the figures on the cross near Whitford in North Wales, the old pre-Christian images were still only just below the surface. Next in date (probably about 825) is the South Cross (figure 48), the decoration of which, as already noted, closely resembles that on St Martin's Cross at Iona. Here, however, instead of the Virgin and Child we find the usual Irish representation of the Crucifixion on the west face.

The finest of the crosses at Clonmacnois, with which only the Cross of Muiredach at Monasterboice can compare, is the Cross of the Scriptures, which stands on the west side near the entrance to the cathedral ruins. It is also called Flann's Cross since the inscription at the foot of the shaft probably commemorates King Flann, who died in 916, and Colman, an abbot of Clonmacnois, who died in 921. Both are thought to be represented above the inscription, where there are two figures apparently setting up a cross (or planting the corner post of a building). In the ring above is Christ in Glory, dominating the whole cross (see figure 49). Normally the stone ring on the Irish high crosses consists of four quadrants linking the arms, but in this magnificent example the whole ring has been brought forward to cover the arms and it is further enriched with decorative roundels and small circular projections on the inside of the ring. On the top of the cross is a 'house-cap' showing in miniature the appearance of a Celtic oratory or shrine. Taken as a whole, it is clear that the purpose of this cross was only partly commemorative; it was chiefly designed to act as a preaching point or 'sermon in stone'.

The conception of the 'sermon in stone' reached its fullest expression at Monasterboice in County Louth. Both the surviving crosses at Monasterboice have biblical scenes covering every surface and yet the form of the cross gives all this detail an artistic and iconographic unity. There is a real sense in which each of these crosses is best appreciated as a single whole, without at first analysing the detail, and from whichever angle they are viewed

50. West Cross, Monasterboice, County Louth.

there is something to be learnt. The West Cross near the tower is the tallest of all the high crosses in Ireland, measuring about 22 feet (6.7 metres) in height (see figure 50). An interesting feature of this cross is that the block of stone from which its arms were carved is much better preserved than the house-cap above it and the shaft below it. The figural style on the head and shaft appears to be the same and one can only conclude that either this particular block was of better quality stone or that it was replaced some time later by the same school of sculptors. The Crucifixion scene on this better preserved section appears to be of a later type (with Christ's head drooping to one side) than that shown on the Cross of Muiredach.

The Cross of Muiredach itself (see cover photograph) is so called after the inscription to an abbot of that name who died in 922, which appears on the lowest part of the shaft on the west side. It is 18 feet (5.5 metres) high and, like the Cross of the Scriptures at Clonmacnois, the head and shaft are carved from a single block of stone, with base and house-cap adding to the overall height. The figures are carved in bold relief and are remarkably well preserved. The scenes on the two main faces should be read from the bottom up. On the west face the shaft has three panels showing the arrest of Christ, followed by Thomas putting his hand into Christ's wound, and then Christ giving a key to Peter and a book to Paul, with the Crucifixion in the circle of the head above. On the east face, the lowest scene on the shaft is of Adam and Eve with Cain and Abel, followed by David and Goliath, Moses striking the rock and the wise men adoring the infant Jesus. In the circle of the head above is the figure of Christ in Majesty, holding a cross and sceptre, as on the Cross of the Scriptures, but with more detail. There is the figure of the archangel Michael weighing the souls and preventing a demon from pulling down the scales, while on the right the lost souls are driven away and on the left those who are saved, led by David and musicians, face towards the Risen Lord.

In this way the Old and New Testaments were brought together, and fully developed concepts of the Crucifixion and Resurrection were expressed in one coherent composition. Here we see the Victorious Christ, as depicted in the late classical sculpture of Italy and Gaul and crudely represented by the circular cross-forms of the earliest Christian monuments in Celtic Britain. The high crosses of Ireland were designed to proclaim the same message.

5
Gazetteer

Places with monuments mentioned in this book, with grid references.

Cornwall

Cardinham. SX 123687

Doniert's Stone, near St Cleer. SX 237688

Lanherne, near St Mawgan. SW 872659

Perranporth. SW 773564

St Buryan. SW 409258

Sancreed. SW 421295

Ireland

Ahenny, County Tipperary. S 413291

Carndonagh, County Donegal. C 463459

Castledermot, County Kildare. S 783849

Clonmacnois, County Offaly. N 010308. Good collection of early Christian stones

Duvillaun, County Mayo. F 581161

Fahan, County Donegal. C 345263

Gallen Priory, County Offaly. N 116235

Glendalough, County Wicklow. T 123968. Good collection of early Christian stones

Inishkea North, County Mayo. F 567225

Kells, County Meath. N 740759

Monasterboice, County Louth. O 043821

Moone, County Kildare. S 789927

Reask, County Kerry. Q 367044

Isle of Man

Calf of Man (Crucifixion slab), now in the Manx Museum, Douglas.

Lonan cross-slab, near Ballamenaugh. SC 427794

Maughold. SC 492918. Major collection of carved stones in the churchyard.

Onchan. SC 400782.

Scotland

Aberlemno, Tayside. NO 522555

Barochan cross, now in Paisley Abbey, Strathclyde. NS 485639

Camustone, near Monikie, Tayside. NO 519379

Dunfallandy, Tayside. NN 946565

Dupplin cross, near Forteviot, Tayside. NO 050189

Govan, Strathclyde. NS 553658. Large and important collection of early Christian stones.

Hamilton, Strathclyde. NS 723555

Hilton of Cadboll cross-slab, now in the Royal Museum of Scotland.

Iona, Strathclyde. NM 286245. Fragments of early Christian crosses, cross-marked stones and later West Highland sculpture in the Abbey museum.

Keills, Strathclyde. NR 691805. Early Christian stones and West Highland sculpture in the converted chapel.

Kildalton, Islay, Strathclyde. NR 458508

Kilmartin, Strathclyde. NR 834988

Kilmory Knap, Strathclyde. NR 702751. Early Christian stones and West Highland sculpture in the converted chapel.

Kirkmadrine, Galloway. NX 080483

Meigle, near Alyth, Tayside. NO 287445. Important collection of Pictish cross-slabs.

Nigg, Highland. NH 804717.

Over Kirkhope pillar-stone, now in the Royal Museum of Scotland.

Riasg Buidhe, Colonsay, Strathclyde. NR 395968.

Rossie Priory, Tayside. NO 291308

Ruthwell, Dumfriesshire. NY 100682

St Andrews, Fife. NO 513166. Large collection of early Christian stones in the cathedral.

St Vigeans, Tayside. NO 638429. Important collection of Pictish cross-slabs.

Shandwick, Highland. NH 855747.
Sueno's Stone, near Forres, Grampian. NJ 046595.
Whithorn, Galloway. NX 444403. Early Christian stones and crosses of the later Whithorn school in Whithorn Museum.

Wales
Carew, Dyfed. SN 046037
Laugharne, Dyfed. SN 302115.
Llandough, South Glamorgan. ST 168733.
Llangan, South Glamorgan. SS 958778.
Llangeinwen, near Dwyran, Anglesey, Gwynedd. SH 439658.
Llangernyw, Clwyd. SH 876675.
Llanrhaiadr-ym-Mochnant, Clwyd. SJ 124261.
Llantwit Major, South Glamorgan. SS 966687. Collection of early Christian stones inside the church.
Llanynys cross, now in Brecknock Museum.

Llowes, Powys. SO 193418.
Llywel stone, now in the British Museum.
Maen Achwyfan, near Whitford, Clwyd. SJ 129787.
Margam, West Glamorgan. SS 802863. Large collection of early Christian stones in the museum adjoining Margam Abbey.
Meifod, Powys. SJ 155132.
Merthyr Mawr, Mid Glamorgan. SS 883776.
Nevern, Dyfed. SN 083401.
Penally, Dyfed. SS 117992.
Penmachno, Gwynedd. SH 790505.
Penmon Priory, Anglesey, Gwynedd. SH 631808. Two major crosses.
Pillar of Eliseg, near Llangollen, Clwyd. SJ 203446.
St Davids, Dyfed. SM 752254. Early Christian stones in the cathedral.
Tregaron pillar-stone, now in the National Museum of Wales.

6
Museums

Ireland
National Museum of Ireland, Kildare Street, Dublin 2. Telephone: 01 618811. Few sculptured pieces on display but the general background of early Irish art is well illustrated.

Isle of Man
Manx Museum, Douglas. Telephone: 0624 675522. The Calf of Man Crucifixion and general background.

Scotland
Royal Museum of Scotland, Queen Street, Edinburgh EH2 1JD. Telephone: 031-225 7534. Large and informative display.

Wales
Brecknock Museum, Captain's Walk, Brecon, Powys LD3 7DW. Telephone: 0874 624121. Small number of important stones.
National Museum of Wales, Cathays Park, Cardiff CF1 3NP. Telephone: 0222 397951. Gallery of early Christian carved stones and crosses.

7
Further reading

General

Laing, Lloyd and Jennifer. *A Guide to the Dark Age Remains in Britain.* Constable, 1979.

Megaw, Ruth and Vincent. *Celtic Art.* Thames & Hudson, 1989.

Schiller, Gertrud. *Iconography of Christian Art*, volume 2 'The Passion of Jesus Christ'. Lund Humphries, 1972.

Thomas, Charles. *Christianity in Roman Britain to AD 500.* Batsford, 1981.

Thomas, Charles. *Celtic Britain.* Thames & Hudson, 1986.

Cornwall

Okasha, Elisabeth. *Corpus of Early Christian Inscribed Stones of South-west Britain.* Leicester University Press, 1993.

Thomas, Charles. 'Ninth Century Sculpture in Cornwall: a Note' in J. Lang (editor), *Anglo-Saxon and Viking Age Sculpture.* British Archaeological Reports (British Series) 49 (1978), 75-83.

Ireland

Edwards, Nancy. *The Archaeology of Early Medieval Ireland.* Batsford, 1990.

Hamlin, Ann. *Historic Monuments of Northern Ireland.* Department of Environment, Belfast, 1987.

Harbison, Peter. *Pilgrimage in Ireland.* Barrie & Jenkins, 1991.

Harbison, Peter. 'A Group of Early Christian Carved Stones in County Donegal' in John Higgitt (editor), *Early Medieval Sculpture in Britain and Ireland.* British Archaeological Reports (British Series) 152 (1986), 49-85.

Henry, Françoise. *Irish Art in the Early Christian Period.* Methuen, 1965.

Henry, Françoise. *Irish Art during the Viking Invasions.* Methuen, 1967.

Higgins, J. G. *The Early Christian Cross Slabs, Pillar Stones and Related Monuments of County Galway, Ireland.* British Archaeological Reports (International Series) 375, 1987.

Richardson, Hilary, and Scarry, John. *An Introduction to Irish High Crosses.* The Mercier Press, Cork, 1990.

Roe, Helen. *The High Crosses of Kells.* Meath Archaeological and Historical Society, 1981.

Roe, Helen. *Monasterboice and Its Monuments.* County Louth Archaeological and Historical Society, 1981.

Isle of Man

Cubbon, A. M. 'The Early Church in the Isle of Man' in S. M. Pearce (editor), *The Early Church in Western Britain and Ireland.* British Archaeological Reports (British Series) 102 (1982), 257-82.

Cubbon, A. M. *The Art of the Manx Crosses.* The Manx Museum and National Trust, Douglas, 1983.

Kinvig, R. H. *The Isle of Man.* Liverpool University Press, 1975.

Scotland

Allen, J. Romilly, and Anderson, Joseph. *The Early Christian Monuments of Scotland.* Reprinted by The Pinkfoot Press, Forfar, Angus, 1993.

Close-Brooks, J., and Stevenson, R. B. K. *Dark Age Sculpture.* National Museum of Antiquities of Scotland, Edinburgh, 1982.

Dunbar, J. G., and Fisher, I. *Iona.* HMSO, 1983.

Henderson, Isabel. *The Picts.* Thames & Hudson, 1967.

Henderson, Isabel. 'Sculpture North of the Forth after the Take-over by the Scots' in J. Lang (editor), *Anglo-Saxon and Viking Age Sculpture.* British Archaeological Reports (British Series) 49 (1978), 47-74.

Laing, Lloyd and Jenny. *The Picts and the Scots.* Alan Sutton, 1993.

Radford, C. A. R., and Donaldson, G. *Whithorn.* HMSO, 1984.

Ritchie, Anna. *Picts.* HMSO, 1989.

Royal Commission on the Ancient and Historical Monuments of Scotland. *Exploring Scotland's Heritage.* HMSO, 1985-7. Eight volumes covering the whole of Scotland.

Wales

Davies, Wendy. *Wales in the Early Middle Ages.* Leicester University Press, 1982.

Edwards, Nancy, and Lane, Alan (editors). *The Early Church in Wales and the West.* Oxbow Monograph 16, 1992.

Nash-Williams, V. E. *The Early Christian Monuments of Wales.* University of Wales Press, 1950.

Redknap, Mark. *The Christian Celts.* National Museum of Wales, 1991.

Royal Commission on Ancient and Historical Monuments in Wales. *An Inventory of Ancient Monuments in Glamorgan*, volume 1, part 3. HMSO, 1976.

Index

Page numbers in italics refer to illustrations